# A Revelation of the Lamb for America

### Sandy Davis Kirk, Ph.D.

McDougal Publishing is a ministry of The McDougal Foundation, Inc., a Maryland nonprofit corporation dedicated to spreading the Gospel of the Lord Jesus Christ to as many people as possible in the shortest time possible.

Published by:

# McDougal Publishing

P.O. Box 3595
Hagerstown, MD 21742-3595
www.mcdougalpublishing.com

ISBN 1-58158-063-0

Printed in the United States of America
For Worldwide Distribution

# *Dedication*

To my students: When I saw your passion, it thrilled me; when I felt your pain, it broke me; but when I watched you open your hearts to receive a *revelation of the Lamb*, my heart completely melted. To you, my beloved students at Brownsville Revival School of Ministry, I dedicate this book.

I believe Jesus looks down and weeps tears of joy over what He sees in you. For now you — a John the Baptist generation — will call America and all the world to look up and behold the Lamb. Then, at long last, the Father will be satisfied, for His Son will receive the glory He deserves for giving Himself as the Lamb.

# Acknowledgments

When Heaven opens in revival and the Spirit of God sweeps in like a soft summer breeze, visions, songs, prophecies, books and other creative works pour into people's hearts. This book is simply a response to a word the Lord uttered in the midst of revival.

I am forever grateful to Pastor John Kilpatrick for his shepherding of revival and his constant love for the presence of God. I am thankful too for Lindell Cooley's Davidic worship, for Chaplain Robertson's superintending guidance, for Pastor Richard Crisco's warmhearted and passionate leadership, and for Dr. Larry Martin's anointing and teaching ability.

I am equally grateful for this wonderful church, Brownsville Assembly of God in Pensacola, for you pursued the Lord until He came and now the heavens are open for us to receive a revelation of God's Son as the Lamb.

# Contents

# Foreword by
# Pastor John Kilpatrick

The hallmark of the Brownsville Revival from the beginning has been souls and repentance. Night after night, the Holy Spirit would draw thousands from all over the world. There was and still is an acute awareness of God's holiness. This generation is ready to be confronted with a fresh revelation of Calvary. The Body of Christ worldwide has strayed from its message of the Lamb slain from the foundation of the world.

In her new book, Dr. Sandy Kirk has a special anointing that God has given her to once again bring into clear focus what Christianity is all about. When I read her manuscript, I knew it was a work that would bring glory to God and also sow seeds of repentance in anyone privileged to read *A Revelation of the Lamb for America*.

In the aftermath of September 11, 2001, our nation has desperately searched for answers. America was shocked into the reality of how quickly everything can change—everything, that is, except one thing: the timeless, changeless message of God's Lamb, provided as a sacrifice for a lost and dying world. From the crucible of human experiences related to our national tragedy, Sandy extracts some beautiful parallels that lead you to recognize immediately that the Holy Spirit inspired this book so we can behold the Lamb in even greater dimensions.

I have the privilege of being Dr. Kirk's pastor, and she also serves as an instructor on the faculty of Brownsville Revival School of Ministry here in Pensacola. Her tender spirit, as well as her outstanding educational skills, have endeared her to our students and staff. I believe when you read this book and conclude the final pages, you will have a fresh look at heroism and patriotism, but even more importantly, a fresh appreciation of God's amazing grace. Get ready to see new possibilities in your everyday journey with God. You never know what a day will bring!

# Introduction: America's Need

One terrifying thought fills the young soldier's mind: *What will she think when she sees my face?* As a prisoner of war in a German prison camp, Private Joe Cohen's face had been burned so badly the Germans had let him go. Now he stands, dressed in crisp uniform, his back to the audience as he and several other heroes receive the Distinguished Service Cross.

As the medal of honor is pinned upon his jacket, paralyzing thoughts crowd his mind. He hears only phrases of the praise heaped upon him: "For extraordinary heroism against the enemy ... with complete disregard for his own safety ... reflects great credit on himself and the Armed Forces ... ."

He had begged, even ordered, his girl not to come. He wanted to wait until enough plastic surgery had been performed that she could bear to look at his face. But she never promised, and now he wonders if somewhere out there in the sea of people gathered for the ceremony could be the girl he loves.

The ceremony ends. People shake the hero's hand, but he hardly notices. His eyes scan restlessly, searching, longing. Then suddenly three people break from the crowd: Joe's parents and the girl. She smiles as she runs toward the platform. Instinctively, almost forgetting his face, he races toward her.

They meet in the middle of the auditorium. Hundreds of eyes watch, but the two are unaware. The girl looks straight into Joe's flaming red, malformed face. She never flinches. Throwing her arms around him, she cries over and over again, "Joe! Joe! Joe! You're the most beautiful man in the whole world!"[1]

I want to show you now another Man who is even more beautiful. Though His face has been mutilated and scarred, we need to look at His bleeding face without flinching. Though everything within us cringes from the sight of blood, though we shrink from watching the whip plow His flesh and the nails pierce His hands, we need to look until we can see.

Though He is marred almost beyond recognition, if we will look, something inside us will soften. Our hearts will melt. Our pain will ease. Our purpose will be restored. Our passion will rekindle. Our wounds will heal.

The heart of America broke on September 11, 2001. The attacks of terrorism, killing thousands of innocent people in our homeland, tore a gaping hole in the fabric of the nation. This is why America needs *a revelation of the Lamb*. We need to see the God who knows how it feels to be torn from those He loves. We need to know the One who understands the anguish of gut-wrenching emotions, who knows the feeling of a tear welling up in His eye and sliding down His cheek.

We need to know the side of God that preachers often fail to disclose. We need to see the God who stepped down from Heaven to walk as one of us on earth. We need to know a God who loves to be near us, who smiles and laughs and giggles with us, a God who delights in filling us with His love and breathing His presence into our weary hearts. We need *a revelation of the Lamb*, for wounds scar the soul of America. We need the breath of Heaven blowing down upon us, giving us hope, rekindling our joy, our purpose, our passion. We need to inhale the freshness of the presence of God. We need to feel the warm oil of His Spirit pouring into our wounds.

So I call you now to look, really look — perhaps even for the very first time — at Jesus, the Lamb of God. See the Man who offered himself as the Lamb — sweating, bleeding, weeping, loving, healing, crying, dying, shining.

Though it hurts to look, don't flinch. Open wide your heart and see beyond the bloody wounds and mutilated flesh. Look until, like the soldier's girl, you can cry with all your heart, "Jesus, You truly are the most beautiful Man in the world!"

*Sandy Davis Kirk*
*Pensacola, Florida*

Endnote:

1. Adapted from a story by I. Kaufman, condensed from *American Jews in World War II*; cited in Jack Canfield, Mark Victor Hansen and Sidney R. Slagter, compilers, "The Most Beautiful Man in the World," in *Chicken Soup for the Veteran's Soul* (Deerfield Beach, FL: Health Communications, Inc., 2001), pp. 237-241.

*One*

# A Revelation of the Lamb

The moment my knees hit the floor at the altar in Brownsville's chapel, the Holy Spirit flooded me. He spoke to me clearly with a sense of earnest passion. The words He spoke impelled me to write this book, urging Christians everywhere to consider this plea from Heaven.

Before I tell you what the Holy Spirit said, let me explain the background. Three days before, terrorists had struck the Twin Towers in New York City and the Pentagon in Washington, D.C., and President Bush had called the nation to pray. We were meeting for our morning chapel service at the Brownsville Revival School of Ministry in Pensacola, where I teach. A special noon prayer meeting would follow the morning chapel and classes.

On my way to chapel, while driving from our camp along the country road and over the bridge leading into Pensacola, thoughts stirred in my mind. The whole nation still reeled in shock and grief. A sense of fear seemed to grip most Americans, no one knowing where terrorism might strike next.

Just that morning I had watched a prominent evangelist on a news program. When asked how a merciful God could allow such a disaster, he boldly expressed the Gospel. He said that all have sinned and fallen short of God's glory. He explained that God gave His only Son on a cross so that we would be forgiven and cleansed of our sin.

His simple message rang with truth, but it seemed to go right over the heads of the commentators. I had the feeling it missed the target for which it was intended — the millions of unsaved people who want God but don't know how to find Him.

I had been puzzling over this as I drove to chapel that morning. Something seemed to be missing from the evangelist's words, but what? His message was typical of any good Gospel presentation. Yet, somehow it seemed mechanical, rote, void of heart-gripping power. Why did it seem to lack something? What was missing?

Many Americans have been inoculated against the Gospel. They've heard the message so many times that it doesn't sink in. But why are we so jaded that we cannot seem to hear? Why do we yawn and wipe the sleep from our eyes whenever the story is told? Why are we bored with a message that cost our Lord so much?

These were the questions rolling over in my mind on my way to chapel. I finally reached the ministry school and eased into the parking lot. I slipped into the chapel and headed straight for the altar. The moment my knees struck the floor, the Holy Spirit flooded me. He said, "America needs *a revelation of the Lamb!*"

His words burned into my heart. The message was simple, but it hit my spirit with force. I trembled under the power of His presence. I listened with my heart as He unfolded to me again the revelation of the Lamb.

When He had finished, I stood up and worshiped. All around me students and faculty paced the floor, crying out to God in prayer. Songs from the worship team filled the air. Tears spilled shamelessly, and faces flushed in passion. Veins bulged in necks, and voices were lifted fervently toward Heaven. We were all desperate for God in the midst of this national crisis.

But I was only vaguely aware of my surroundings, so caught up was I in the presence of God. My face burned with the light of His face, and my body vibrated under the power of the word the Holy Spirit had just exploded in my heart: "America needs *a revelation of the Lamb!*"

Finally, I stumbled over to a pew and grabbed a pen. As fast as my fingers could race, I wrote down everything the Lord was showing me about this desperate need of America.

After chapel I poured out my heart in my Systematic Theology class, telling my students why

America needs *a revelation of the Lamb*. Later, in our noon prayer meeting, I delivered my soul to the entire student body. Now, I want to pour out my heart to you through the pages of this book.

I told this story in condensed form in the last chapter of my book *America Ablaze*. Now I want to give you the entire message, combined with true stories of patriotism and heroism.

## *America, Lift Up Your Head!*

A.W. Tozer said, "What the Church needs to regain her lost power is to see Heaven opened and have a transforming vision of God."[1] That's what America needs, as well.

In fact, this is what Jesus said to do when nations are in anguish: *"LOOK UP AND LIFT UP YOUR HEADS"* (Luke 21:28, AMP). So what if, right now, America would lift up her head and look into Heaven? What would she see? What would you see if suddenly Heaven opened, and you could see Jesus? How would He look?

John the Apostle told us in his Revelation what our eyes would behold: *"And there between the throne and the four living creatures ... I SAW A LAMB standing, as though it had been slain"* (Revelation 5:6, AMP).

Does this make you think of a fluffy white lamb? Oh, no! The reason John describes Jesus as looking like a Lamb is because He still bears the wounds of His sacrifice. He's in the form of a Man, but deep holes still mar His flesh — as the hymn says — "rich wounds, yet visible above, in beauty glorified."[2]

Ordinarily, wounds heal with passing time, but not these wounds. Jesus' wounds are supernatural. Charles Spurgeon said that those wounds are "lustrous with supernal splendor."[3] These are more than mere scars. They are like medals of glory, still embedded in His body and announcing the message of His grand sacrifice on the cross.

That's why, after Jesus rose, He pulled back His robe and threw open His hands to display the wounds in His flesh. He wanted His disciples to see that He still was bearing wounds like a slain lamb.

In the pages that follow, you will look again at the Lamb. I want you to look until you can see, with the eyes of your heart, the crimson streams draining from His wounds, until you can feel the tears dripping from His eyes, until you experience the power streaming out from the wounds of the Lamb.

You see, there is power in beholding the Lamb. A story explains it well:

## Power in Beholding the Lamb

A fifteen-year-old boy blindly trudged through a snowstorm, heading toward a Baptist church in the village. The snow froze his face and stung his eyes, but he was desperate to get to church. He knew he was unsaved, but somehow he wanted to find God.

Finally, he realized he couldn't make it to the village, so he stopped at a little Primitive Methodist chapel along the way. He had heard that these Methodists shouted so loudly it made one's head ache, but he didn't care. He had to find God. He slipped into the back pew and waited for the service to begin.

It was the first Sunday of January, 1850, and the regular minister of this church in England was snow-bound. An old country man, speaking in crude language, stood to preach the sermon. "The Bible says, *'Look to me and be saved, all the ends of the earth,'* " the old man said. Then, lifting up his voice, he shouted, "So look up now ... . Lift yer eyes and see yer Savior bleedin' and dyin' on a cross. See the blood drippin' down from His wounds."

He continued, "Look up at Jesus! See Him dyin' on the cross. Now see Him risin' from the dead and ascendin' up to Heaven. See Him sittin' down upon a throne." Then the old man leaned over his pulpit and pointed straight at the fifteen-year-old boy on the back pew. "Young man, you are miserable, and you will be miserable until you obey this Scripture — look to Him and be saved!" Suddenly the boy's spiritual eyes opened and he looked up. He saw the Lamb, and in that moment, young Charles Spurgeon was saved!

Spurgeon later became known as "the Prince of Preachers," but he always looked back to that moment when he gazed on the bleeding Savior and was saved. He said:

*E'er since by faith I saw the stream*
*Thy flowing wounds supply,*
*Redeeming love has been my theme*
*And shall be till I die.*[4]

Because of this transforming look, for the rest of his life Charles Spurgeon made it his life's purpose to give *a revelation of the Lamb* to his generation. Today, even as John the Baptist cried, "Behold the Lamb of God!" the Holy Spirit calls a John the Baptist generation to give *a revelation of the Lamb* to America.

Perhaps this is why we seem to have so many shallow conversions in America. Maybe the reason so many slide back into sin or get stuck in dry religion is because we haven't given them a true revelation of the Lamb. Spurgeon said, "There is no true, deep, tender, living conversion except through the cross."[5] That's why it's time for us Christians to humble ourselves and simply lift up the Lamb.

So now I invite you to come look with all your heart and soul at Jesus. Look until the message of Calvary burns into the fleshy tablet of your heart, causing it to melt beneath the heat.

Come look up at Jesus until you see the tears pooling in His eyes and swimming down His cheeks. Gaze at Him until you can almost reach up and touch the wet drops of blood spilling from open wounds.

Come draw so near this blazing bush that you can feel the heat flickering against your face. Come look until you can feel the presence of God breathing down upon you.

Breathe in the richness of His presence until you are *"wholly filled and flooded with God Himself"* (Ephesians 3:19, AMP). Let Him fill the deep, hurting, hungry places in your soul. Let Him fill you so full that you are able to unveil to America a grand revelation of the Lamb.

Endnotes:

1. A.W. Tozer, *The Knowledge of the Holy: The Attributes of God: Their Meaning in the Christian Life* (San Francisco: Harper & Row Publishers, 1961), p. 121.
2. "Crown Him With Many Crowns," by Matthew Bridges.
3. Charles Spurgeon, "Mourning at the Sight of the Crucified," in *The Power of the Cross of Christ*, Lance C. Wubbels, comp. (Lynnwood, WA: Emerald Books, 1995), p. 190.
4. Lewis Drummond, *Spurgeon, Prince of Preachers* (Grand Rapids, MI: Kregel Publications, 1992), p. 113.
5. Charles Spurgeon, "The Marvelous Magnet," in *The Power of the Cross of Christ*, p. 21

# Two

# The Scars and Stripes
# of the Lamb

Soldiers watch in solemn respect as a long line of United Nations prisoners of war stagger across "Freedom Bridge" at the end of the Korean War. One young man, his eyes dull and his face gray, drags his emaciated body over the bridge. At one point, he stumbles into the railing of the bridge. Every eye focuses on the bony-armed, stick-like figure of a man, now with lines of suffering scribbled across his face. Rushing to his side, an MP major tries to help, but the gallant soldier waves him away. The soldier's eyes are focused on something ahead. He wants no one to help him.

There it is just across the bridge — held high as a valiant symbol of freedom — the American flag. The

27

young soldier fixes his eyes on the Stars and Stripes, unfurled and lifted on a pole. With every ounce of strength in his body, he hobbles toward the flag.

He shuffles faster now, finally reaching it. Suddenly, he falls to his knees, trembling. He reaches up and tugs at the flag. The flag bearer lowers it, and the soldier buries his face in the red and white stripes, sobbing and shaking uncontrollably.

Every man fights to choke back his emotions. Throats tighten, and tears stream down each face. The silence is deafening. Finally the MP, his cheeks moist with tears, tenderly picks up this skeleton of a young man and carries him to an ambulance.[1]

## Gaze Upon His Stripes

Like that young man who smothered himself in the Stars and Stripes, we need to crawl up close to the One who bears deep red scars and stripes in His own flesh. Like the soldier, we as a nation need to fall to our knees, trembling.

We need to reach up and take His nail-pierced

hands, and then, like the young soldier, we need to bury our faces in His wounds. Even as John the Apostle laid his head upon the Savior's breast, we need to nestle up close to Him and rest our faces against His chest. We need to lose ourselves in His love and let the presence of Almighty God fill the wounds in our souls.

So, right now, wherever you are, I call you to lift up your eyes and see. ... Look beyond the ceiling over your head. Gaze higher than the roof. Look into the sky, but look even higher. See beyond the first and second heavens. Lift the eyes of your heart, and as the Spirit of God pulls back the torn veil, gaze into the third Heaven. Look with all your heart at the One upon the throne.

Look up at Jesus. See Him there, still bleeding like a Lamb with fresh wounds from the cross. Remember, His blood ever flows from these open punctures. Look long and deep at these healing red stripes, raked across His flesh. It is from these wounds that a fountain flows. It's a flood tide of cleansing blood.

To see this more clearly, let's return to the day when God the Son was lifted up on a cross. Jesus said, *"And I, if I be lifted up from the earth, will draw all men unto me"* (John 12:32, KJV). There is drawing power in the cross of Christ. It's not in the two stakes of wood. The magnetic pull comes from a look at the Lamb.

Can you see Him there? Through the centuries people have referred to a God of weakness dying on a cross, but they don't understand. This is the God of all glory and power who humbled Himself as a Lamb. Now, so that we can be forgiven, He allows His flesh to be ripped and torn and nailed.

Look at Him now. See the thorns jammed into His skull. Watch crimson streams ooze from those holes in His brow, dripping down His face, mixing with tears from His eyes and spit from His enemies.

It's unthinkable, I know, but God is doing this for you. He wants to forgive you and draw you near to Himself. He yearns to enjoy intimate fellowship with you. He is lovesick for a relationship with you.

So don't cringe at the sight of His blood. This substance holds the power to wash away your sins. Watch it flow. See the streams spurt from beneath the nails in His hands and spill down His arms. Watch the bloody wounds in His chest where the Roman flagellum, with its bits of bone and metal, curled around His back and rutted His chest, ripping through layers of human tissue. Now, see the flesh hanging in ribbons from His arms and legs and chest. These are the red stripes through which His healing rivers flow. This is God's eternal blood, the blood that will wash away all sin. As Spurgeon said, "His wounds distilled the richest balm that ever healed a sinner's wound."[2]

## A Soldier's Cleansing

On a faraway battlefield a young soldier lies severely wounded. As his lifeblood soaks into the ground, he keeps thinking, *O God, I'm dying. I'm not ready to meet You. Help me, Lord!*

With his head pressed down in the mud, he feels

the warm blood puddling around his face. Over and over in his mind, he thinks, *What was that Bible verse that my grandfather always told me? "Someday, Son, you'll have to get right with God. When you do, remember this verse,* 'If you confess your sins, He is faithful and just to forgive your sin and cleanse you' "(see 1 John 1:9). *Yes! Yes, that was it!*

Now, even as the life-force drains out, he cries out to God, confessing his sin and asking the blood of Jesus to cleanse him. Peace fills his heart, and he relaxes, losing consciousness.

Days later the soldier awakens in a hospital, surprised to be alive. A medic found him and lifted him by helicopter to safety. Now, as he regains his strength, he knows he is a changed man. Christ has come into his life, even as he thought he was dying.

Oh, sure, maybe this was what some call a "foxhole conversion," but it was still real. That young soldier had been forgiven and the blood of Jesus had washed him perfectly clean. His blood will do the same for you.

Do you need forgiveness? If you do, Jesus longs

to cleanse you. He spilled His blood for this purpose: to wash you and give you a new life.

No matter what you've done, He loves you. He's not angry with AIDS victims and homosexuals. He doesn't hate prostitutes, alcoholics and drug addicts. He doesn't resent you if you've divorced, had an abortion or lost your virginity. He loves you. He yearns for you. He simply wants to draw you near and wash you clean and give you a new life.

So, I invite you, even now, to bow your heart before Him. Tell Him you are sorry for everything that keeps you away from Him, and give Him your whole life.

On the other hand, you may have been a Christian for many years, but I'm talking to you as well. We sometimes get so hardened to sin that we can't see it in ourselves. Sins such as arrogance, pride, judgmentalism, criticism, bitterness, gossip, gluttony, lust and many more creep in and need to be cleansed.

I'll never forget the night I saw the Lord and He exposed my pride and arrogance. I had been through a humiliating experience, which I thought had unjustly hurt my reputation. I went forward for ministry in the revival church which I often attended during seminary. I waited for prayer, and then suddenly I had a vision of the Lord.

He was hanging from a cross, bloody and shamed. People around Him mocked and spit in His face. He hung stripped and beaten. Blood bathed His body.

I heard Him speak, not audibly, but somewhere deep within me. He said, "I became of no reputation for you. Will you be willing to become of no reputation for Me?"

I crumpled to the floor, broken by His brokenness. It was a transforming moment for me. I wept and wept and wept some more, pouring out repentance on His feet. In the light of His humility, I saw my arrogance. I repented of my pride and my desire for dignity and respect. I laid my reputation at His feet, and I have never been the same since that day. It was seeing the scars and the stripes of the Lamb that broke me.

One day during the Korean War, an American soldier saw a house burning with a Korean family inside. Risking the flames, he raced into the house, placed two small children inside his jacket, and charged back out through the flames.

As he fell to the ground, severely burned on his face and hands, the roof of the house caved in, killing the parents. The two children were brought to America and put up for adoption.

Because several people wanted the children, a court was held to decide who were the most fit parents. One couple was wealthy and could offer the children everything an American child could ever hope to have. The other was a poor soldier, returned from the battlefield, with little to offer. After the judge heard the wealthy couple's plea, he turned to the soldier and asked skeptically, "What gives you the right to ask for these two children?"

The soldier didn't speak. He simply stood in the middle of the courtroom and held up his hands, horribly burned and scarred.

Everyone in the room gasped when they saw the scars, obviously received when saving the children's lives. Those scars were like medals of honor. They spoke volumes. Without words, they said, "I bought these children with a price; the cost was my scars."

Many Americans still question, "Why should I give my life to Christ? What gives Him the right to expect me to serve Him?" Jesus doesn't say a word. He simply stands in the court of Heaven and lifts up His hands. He opens His robe and reveals His side. His wounds are like medals of glory. They say to us, "This is the price I paid for you, America. The cost was My scars."

## *Bury Your Heart*

So, I ask you again to look back up at Jesus. Gaze into His face, and look upon the visage, marred and bloodied, and hanging in shame upon a cross. Let His lowliness and humility shine light upon your own heart.

Steve Hill, the evangelist God used to spark the

Brownsville Revival, said, "I believe that deep within every man and woman there exists a fountain just waiting to erupt. It comes from finally seeing the reality of who we are in relation to God and His holiness."[3]

Look deeply then into His pure eyes, and fall at His feet and repent of everything in you that is not like Him. But as you do, know this — the blood of the Lamb makes you perfectly clean.

Wait before Him until you know with all your heart that He has washed away the grime of sin and made you pure as a little child. Now, lift your eyes back up to the Wounded One. See the smile on His face. Feel the love in His heart. See Him beckoning to you. Respond with all your might. Envision yourself crawling up into His lap and resting in His embrace.

Relax in His arms. Lay your face against His chest, the chest so marred with stripes of love. The Bible says, *"By His stripes we are healed"* (Isaiah 53:5), so let the healing love of God flow through His stripes to you. Let Him fill and fill and fill you some more.

Soak your heart in His love. Let it come. Like a sponge in water, take in His goodness. And as His love saturates you, bury your heart forever in the scars and stripes of the Lamb.

Endnotes:

1. "Freedom Village," by James F. Murphy, Jr., 1993; cited in Jack Canfield, Mark V. Hansen and Sidney R. Slagter, *Chicken Soup for the Veteran's Soul,* pp. 2-4.
2. Charles Spurgeon, "The Marvelous Magnet," in *The Power of the Cross of Christ,* p. 20.
3. Stephen Hill, *Time to Weep* (Lake Mary, FL: Creation House, 1997), p. 136.

## Three

# Pierced by the Love of the Lamb

United Flight 93 abruptly veers off course and careens toward Washington, DC. Terrorists, armed with box cutters, have taken over the jet. Women and children on the plane scream. Cell phones jam the airwaves as passengers make last, desperate calls to loved ones. From relatives and friends they learn of other hijacked jets hitting the Pentagon and the World Trade Center.

Now it dawns on the passengers that they have been caught in a massive plot to destroy America. Terrorists have turned their plane into a deadly missile heading toward the Capitol or possibly the White House.

Todd Beamer, one of the passengers, assesses the

situation. After breathing the Lord's Prayer with a telephone operator and leaving a good-bye message for his family, he shouts, "Let's roll!"

Swiftly, he and Jeremy Glick, a 6' 4" judo champion, and a few other men storm the cockpit and overpower the terrorists. In the struggle, the jet plunges earthward and crashes into the Pennsylvania countryside, killing all forty-three passengers on board. But a far greater disaster has been averted.

These men took death upon themselves to save a nation from further destruction. Theirs was an act of profound heroism, and it was born out of courage and love. Perhaps this amazing story can help us understand a little of what God did for us.

We were heading for certain destruction. The terrorism of sin had hijacked our lives, and we were plunging toward death. But then the Lamb — Jesus — stepped down from Heaven. He threw Himself in the way of eternal wrath and died to save us from the punishment we deserve for our sin. It was the ultimate act of heroism, born out of incredible courage and unfathomable love.

So look up again at the Pierced One, dangling from two strips of lumber. But, this time, look beyond the blood and tears. See deeper than the pain and grief. Feel what He must have felt as the sky turned suddenly black. At His birth, it was midnight, and yet the sky was as bright as daytime. Now, at His death, it is midday, and the sky is as dark as midnight.

Watch Jesus as He thrashes on the cross. Something grotesque has fallen upon Him. What is this? Why does He writhe and weep as though under some awful curse. What is happening to Jesus? Surely you know, but have you let the full revelation dawn upon your heart?

Right now, God the Father has taken the sin of the entire human race and poured it into Jesus. No wonder He twists and flails under this grinding weight. Charles Spurgeon said, "Let us abhor the sin that brought such agony upon our beloved Lord. What an accursed thing is the sin that crucified the Lord Jesus!"[1]

Look up at Jesus until your heart trembles with the reality of the sin He bore, for only then can you show America and the nations what Jesus did for them. People need to look until they feel the magnitude of the horrible filth of this sin upon the Lord Jesus. They need to let it grip and squeeze their hearts, until they fall to their knees and cry out to God for forgiveness.

And yet, there's still so much more to see. So look up again at Jesus on the cross. Somehow, let the eyes of your spirit see the unimaginable. Let your heart stretch out to take hold of the meaning of it. Your mind won't be able to grasp this, so let your spirit reach out to grip the dimensions of what happens next.

Suddenly, Jesus stops thrashing. His face whitens, and He appears ghostlike. His eyes fly open wide. His body stiffens. Now what is happening to Jesus? This is more than sin poured down upon Him. Yes, all the sins of the human race have fallen upon Him. He has *"become sin,"* the Bible says (see 2 Corinthians 5:21), but it's even more than this.

True, the Father has turned His face away from

the Son, which is almost incomprehensible. This is the One who lived in intimate, face-to-face fellowship in the bosom of God through all eternity. To cause a separation in this divine union is horrible beyond comprehension. But it's even more than this still. Right now, unseen by human eyes, God the Father — with trembling hand and breaking heart — has tipped the cup of wrath upon His Son.

Now the contents burn down. Like flaming hot lava pouring from the volcano of eternity, the molten wrath and punishment of God blazes down upon the innocent Son.

Please pause for a moment and think about this. This is infinite wrath, condensed into three hours and roaring down on one Man. Furthermore, this is the punishment for all humanity, compacted and poured down upon the Lamb.

Let this soak in deep. Jesus took the punishment of eternal Hell upon Himself — all compressed into three hours, the last three hours of darkness on the cross. And He didn't endure just one person's Hell; He endured all humanity's Hell.

Theologians call this *propitiation*, which means "a sacrifice to avert wrath." Like the passengers on Todd Beamer's plane, who took death upon themselves to save a nation from further destruction, Jesus took wrath and death upon Himself to save us from eternal destruction.

That's why He became a Lamb. Offering Himself before the creation of the world, He took the punishment of Hell upon Himself to give us eternal life. He drank the Father's cup of punishment so that we could be spared the punishment we deserve for sin.

## Infinite Love

How could He do it? Why would He do it? There's really only one reason that God the Son would have endured such punishment. There's only one reason the Father poured the cup upon His Son, breaking His own heart. What is that reason? It is love. God loves you so much that He cannot bear to live without you. He would rather endure your Hell than live in Heaven without you. So He crushes His Son with the punishment you and I deserve.

During all those years when you were playing with sin, Jesus loved you. He cried for you. He longed for you. He wasn't sitting in Heaven with a heavy club, ready to beat you over the head for your sin. No! He was crying out to you, saying "Don't you know I already paid for your sin? I already took your punishment. I already poured out My blood to wash you clean."

So no matter where you are in your spiritual walk with God — whether you've been a Spirit-filled Christian most of your life or you've never known the Lord at all — come to Him now. Look up at Him with all your heart.

See blood spilling down to earth. Look upon the Pierced One, and let Him melt your soul with His love.

Paul prayed that we would somehow experience *"the width and length and depth and height"* of God's love (Ephesians 3:18). Nowhere has the love of God been more vividly displayed than at Calvary, where God's eternal Son took our punishment for sin.

Yet, here in America, we've presented a Lamb-less Gospel. We haven't caused people to see, with the eyes of their hearts, the God who became a Lamb — bleeding, weeping, hurting, crying, loving, thirsting, praying, sighing, dying. We've said that *"all have sinned and fall short of the glory of God"* (Romans 3:23), but we haven't shown them the tender, bleeding Lamb. We haven't caused them to feel His love, experience His pain, see His blood, watch His grief and — most of all — behold the cup of wrath He drank.

Americans don't know that God's only Son endured our punishment for sin. They don't realize that He took our Hell so we could have His Heaven. We've given people a cold, mechanical message, and we've reached their heads, not their hearts. Postmodern generations, however, must be touched not only through their minds, but through their emotions. We must reach their feelings, not just their intellects. We must connect through the heart, not the brain. We must help them to see Jesus until their hearts are melted at His feet.

The cross of the Lamb was the turning point of all human history. It was the crisis of all crises, the hinge, the apex, the sparkling mountain peak of all time. Spurgeon said, "All historians must confess that the turning point of the race is the cross of Christ."[2]

That's why I believe it's time for the Church to lift up the Lamb. Since September 11, 2001, America's heart is more tender. Tommy Tenney says, "There's never been a better time for the Church to stand up and say, 'I see the Lord!' "[3] It's time for Christians to cry, "Behold the Lamb," until the Church, and ultimately all of America, is melted by His love.

Spurgeon said that the piercing of our hearts begins when we look upon the Pierced One. It is just like the Bible says: *"They will look on me, the one they have pierced, and they will mourn for him as one mourns for an only child"* (Zechariah 12:10, NIV). It is time to bring *a revelation of the Lamb* to America, so we can be pierced through and through by His love.

My Systematic Theology class at the Brownsville Revival School of Ministry is really a course on the revelation of the Lamb. Knowing that this is a visual generation, I show hundreds of pictures on a multimedia projector and lace my lessons with clips from videos to help illustrate and inspire. One particular clip from *Saving Private Ryan* seemed to have special impact.

We had been studying Christology (the study of Christ) and had just finished the section on the cross. We saw the Savior's wounds and the blood, but, most of all, we saw the wrath and the cup He drank, as He took our punishment for sin. Then I showed the video clip.

In the movie, Captain Miller, played by Tom Hanks, has led a team of expert soldiers deep into the war zone in Europe. Their mission is to find a young man, the only living son of a mother who had lost all her other sons in the war. Then they must retrieve Private Ryan and send him home.

Finally, they find young Ryan and give him orders to return home. By now all the men on the rescue team have been killed, and Captain Miller sits dying in a pool of blood. Knowing they have given their lives to save this one private, Miller pulls Private Ryan close. With his dying breath he whispers, "Earn this!"

It is a gripping scene, as music plays in the background, and a letter is read to Private Ryan's mother, telling why they are returning her only living son. Through the emotion, one feels the impact of seeing men die to save one human life. I turned off the projector in my classroom and said, "These men spilled their blood to save one man. You have a Savior who spilled His blood to save you. In light of what Jesus did for you, now go out and live a life worthy of this sacrifice!"

So now I want to ask you, "Are the things you're living for worth Christ dying for?" This is the epitaph on the revivalist Leonard Ravenhill's gravestone. We can't "earn this" salvation, but we can live our lives with one grand, burning motive: That the

Lamb might receive the glory He deserves for what He suffered on the cross.

## *The Glory He Deserves*

A true story is told of two young Moravian missionaries who boarded a ship to a distant island. No one had ever returned alive from that island, but they felt compelled to go and share Christ with lost souls. On shore, their families stood weeping, knowing they might never see these two young men again.

Sailors heaved in the anchor, white sails were hoisted, and the ship glided out across the sea. One of the young men stood in the stern of the ship. With tears flooding his eyes and his face lifted heavenward, he shouted out across the waters: "May the Lamb receive His due reward for what He suffered on the cross!"[4] His cry electrified the crowd on shore. They lifted their heads upward, focusing above their own pain and gazing at the Lamb who sacrificed all on the cross.

Now, I ask you to do the same. In humility and love, your heart bursting with passion, simply vow to give others *a revelation of the Lamb*. Lift Him up until the Church and, ultimately, all of America is pierced by the love of the Lamb.

**Endnotes:**

1. Charles Spurgeon, "Lama Sabachthani," in *The Power of the Cross of Christ*, p. 117.
2. Tom Carter, ed., *22,000 Quotations From the Writings of Charles Spurgeon* (Grand Rapids, MI: Baker Book House, 1988), p. 47.
3. Tommy Tenney, on Trinity Broadcasting Network, a daily comment in January 2002.
4. Cited in "Acknowledgments," in Stephen Hill, *Time to Weep*, p. 4.

*Four*

# Never Forsaken by the Lamb

Alarms blared at 8:47 A.M. in firehouses all across lower Manhattan. Firefighter Mike Kehoe threw on his gear and lunged toward his engine. As the truck raced to the Twin Towers, suddenly it slowed, strangely zigzagging toward the scene. As Kehoe jumped from the truck, he saw that the engine driver had been swerving to miss the dead bodies of those who had jumped from windows and now littered the pavement.

Knowing the risk to their own lives, but determined to save as many people as they could, firefighters dove into the black blizzard, racing up the tower stairs. Later, on a park bench, stunned and covered with ash, a man cried, "Those poor firemen. They were coming up when we were going down."

He was right. In less than an hour, more than three hundred firefighters, bent on saving lives, lay buried and crushed beneath the twisted metal and debris at Ground Zero. By that evening, in the ashen twilight, amid heaps of rubble, six firetrucks lay smashed and charred, their "ladders twisted like cheap dinner forks."[1]

And there, working through the night, amid a putrid sixteen acres of destruction, knee-deep in human body parts, surviving firefighters could be seen digging. Desperately they dug, tears wetting their cheeks and mixing with the ashes that covered them. Not only were they digging to unearth people who might still be alive; they were fighting ferociously to find their own fallen brothers, the firefighters smothered beneath the ruins.

Night and day they dug — ten hours, sixteen hours, twenty-four hours. Mayor Rudy Giuliani said, "Even if I told them to stop digging, they wouldn't."[2]

Our rescue workers who were at Ground Zero and the Pentagon still struggle with the emotional trauma of this gruesome experience. No one can be expected to endure the horror of seeing body parts piled up to the knees. One man told of seeing a woman's arm move. He desperately dug through the debris to get to her body, but her arm came off in his hands.

Firefighters had their own boots melted to their feet. A volunteer physician, Mark Cerezin, spent two days caring for the "roasted appendages" of the firemen. After cutting the heavy rubber from their bare feet, he said, "Their boots were melted like marshmallows on a stick."[3]

## God's Compassion for America

But I want to remind you again of another Hero who braved the flames and gave His life. The flames He endured were even more intense than the physical elements of fire. They were the flames of eternal wrath, the very blaze of Hell.

The tower was His cross. The dust of darkness came when the sun hid its face. The blood spilling into the ground was His own. There has never been a greater sacrifice on the face of this earth.

That's why Jesus Christ feels the pain of our nation so deeply. He understands America's broken heart. He already experienced for Himself every falling tear, every sob of grief, every pang of horror. He's not a remote, far-off, nebulous, unfeeling God. He's the God who feels our pain with infinite compassion. He's the God who knows the wetness of warm tears soaking His cheeks, mixing, not with ash, but with human spittle.

Yet people still ask, "Where was God on September 11? How could He forsake us like this?" If this is what you've heard or wondered yourself, come with me again to Calvary to see God's answer to human suffering.

## "Why Have You Forsaken Me?"

Look back up to Jesus on the cross to see the rest of the story. For almost three hours now, from the moment darkness fell upon Him at the sixth hour

(12:00 NOON) until the ninth hour (3:00 P.M.), He has been drinking the Father's cup. Wave after wave of divine wrath against sin has crashed down over the innocent Lamb of God.

Watch now as He finally drains the last bitter drop of the cup. See Him push down hard on the nail in His feet to lift His lungs for air. The wound tears open and fresh blood spills to the ground.

Now He prepares to wail the fourth cry from the cross. The first three hours He spoke three times, but in these last three hours He hasn't spoken a word. He couldn't. The horror of drinking the cup has crushed His breath from Him.

As He prepares to speak, look into His eyes. They brim with tears. They ache with anguish. Can you see the look of terror in His eyes? This is the One who lived in intimacy with His Father through all eternity. Now that fellowship has been broken, and He has been punished over and over and over again for sin.

Now He lifts up His voice and screams out through the universe: *"Eli, Eli, lama sabachthani?"*

meaning, *"My God, My God, why have You forsaken me?"* (Matthew 27:46).

## *Has God Forsaken America?*

Do you know what this means? God the Son was forsaken by His Father so that you would never be forsaken by God. Jesus was forsaken so that America, if she turns back to God, would never be forsaken by Father God.

You see, all those tears you've cried alone, Jesus saw. He heard every cry of every person being crushed and torn beneath the debris of the falling towers. He saw every tear, every cry of grief, every drop of American blood dripping into the ground. He saw it. He felt it. He hurt with everyone who was injured. He grieved with all who lost a loved one in this violent act. Every fiber of His being longs to reach out to you and wipe away your tears.

Even if you personally lost no one in the tragedy of September 11, He cares about every tear you've ever cried for any other reason. He saw you when you drove aimlessly through the city, screaming out in pain. He heard you stifling your cries in private, weeping all alone. He knows how you feel. He hurts with you. He aches to draw you near and soothe away the pain. He yearns to fill your life with joy like you've never known.

That's why Jesus went to a cross. That's why He took your sin and endured your punishment for sin. He saw how sin, whether yours or another's, would scar your life. He saw the pain that would come upon this world when people would reject His love, allowing hatred and violence to drive them.

He saw families splitting, children weeping, unborn babies with human souls being slaughtered and discarded. He saw adults violating children and teenagers. He saw wives abandoning husbands and men beating their wives and kicking them aside like pieces of trash. He saw racial wounds still bleeding and teenagers raging. He saw the pain. He felt the heartache. He caught every tear in the palm of His hand.

But that's why He drank the cup and cried this

horrific cry, *"My God, My God, why have You forsaken Me?"* Jesus was forsaken so that you would never be forsaken by God. Never!

That's why His Word says, *"Never will I leave you. Never will I forsake you"* (Hebrews 13:5, NIV). In fact, to be sure we would grasp this, He concluded the book of Matthew with this great promise: *"And surely I am with you always, to the very end of the age"* (Matthew 28:20, NIV).

Sadly, however, many people in America today feel forsaken by God. Pundits and talk show hosts often ask, "How could God abandon our country? Where was God on 9/11?" These are the wrong questions. The question is not how could God forsake America, but how could America forsake God?

We cannot continue to wink at sin and call it "fun" or "freedom." Sin crucified the Savior. Because God made such a monumental sacrifice for us, we cannot continue to reject His Son. We cannot shrink from speaking the name of Jesus in the public square of America. We cannot stand by as Americans spit in the face of the One who loves us so much He bleeds.

Before September 11, our heroes were sports fig-
ures and movie stars. After 9/11, our heroes became
the quiet, rugged men and women who cared more
for others than for their own lives.

When I first walked through an airport after the
attack on America, uniformed soldiers stood, weap-
ons poised over their shoulders. I turned to one and
said, "Thank you for protecting us," then I burst into
tears. My reaction surprised me, but when I thanked
another soldier at the next airport, the same thing
happened. Waves of emotion, capped with inex-
pressible gratitude, swept over me. I wanted to hug
every military man or woman and say, "Thank you
for laying your life on the line to protect our nation."

One Sunday morning in a Catholic church in New
York's upper east side, another group of America's
new heroes was honored. Firefighters from the East
85th Street Station solemnly carried bread and wine
to the altar for communion. The air was charged
with emotion. Tears stung the eyes of every parish-

ioner as they partook of the elements. People fought to swallow their feelings.

These were some of the men who had first arrived on the scene and braved the flames of the falling towers on September 11. Everyone was grimly aware of the firefighters from this brigade who were among the missing.

As these heroes headed down the aisle of the church to leave, the people, most of them sobbing, leapt to their feet, exploding into a long, loud, emotional ovation.

## The Ultimate Hero

There is indeed another Hero who deserves an endless ovation of praise. He's the ultimate Firefighter, for He endured the flames of eternal wrath on the cross. Yet most of us have never really taken the time to express our gratitude to Him. We've never paused to thank Him for taking the punishment we deserve for sin.

Dave Roever, one of America's true heroes from

Vietnam, tells the heartbreaking story of a man near his bed in the hospital. Every inch of his skin had been burned and blown off in Vietnam. Bandages covered him from head to foot.

One day his young wife came into the hospital room to visit him. She took one look and was sickened. She callously pulled off her wedding ring and flipped it onto the bed. "I couldn't walk down the street with you," she said coldly. "You're embarrassing!" He died a few days later.[5]

But that is how most of us have treated our bloody Bridegroom, wounded from head to foot, scarred over His entire body, forsaken by God and man. Most of us have cried more tears over the deaths of our dogs than over the death of our God.

This is why it's time to lift up the Lamb — the Ultimate Hero of all the nations of this earth. It's time to graphically describe what He did for us on the cross. When people blame Him for 9/11, tell them about the flesh that was ripped to bloody shreds. Give them a view of the cup of flaming wrath. Let them hear Jesus bellowing from the cross, *"My God,*

*My God, why have You forsaken Me?"* Help them understand that He was forsaken so that they would never have to be forsaken by God.

I pray, as you close this chapter, that you will fall on your knees and look up to the Lamb of God. Promise Him that for the rest of your life you will thank Him for His supreme sacrifice.

And most of all — no matter what you go through in life, even if America shakes and more towers fall — may you always remember that you can never, never, never be forsaken by your Lamb.

**Endnotes:**

1. Jodie Morse, "Glory in the Glare," *TIME* magazine, December 31, 2002, pp. 95-96.
2. Sally Jenkins, "Company of Heroes," in *America Out of the Ashes* (Tulsa: Honor Books, 2001), p. 64.
3. Sally Jenkins, "Company of Heroes," in *America Out of the Ashes*, p. 65.
4. Sally Jenkins, "Company of Heroes," in *America Out of the Ashes*, p. 60.
5. Dave Roever, *Scars That Heal*, Worldwide Pictures, Inc., 1993, a video presentation.

# Five

# The Beautiful Lamb

A blind Vietnam veteran lingers outside the lounge at a veterans' convention in Los Angeles in 1987. Not wanting to interfere, he quietly stands alone with his Seeing Eye dog, waiting for Colonel Maggie, a hero to many of the vets. Someone finally tells Maggie about the blind man. She strides up to the vet and asks, "What's up, Soldier? You wanted to see me?"

"Yes, Ma'am." Then he explains his story from his war experience, which he had waited twenty years to tell. "Colonel Maggie, when I was hit, you stayed with me in that foxhole, holding me, singing to me, till the medevac came. I wasn't so scared with you there and all."

Then, his voice cracking, he says, "When the doc

went to bandage my eyes, you stopped him. You looked me right in the eyes and told me, 'Someday we'll see each other again.' "

The soldier goes on to tell Maggie how the doctors told him he would never see again. "I wasn't depressed. I knew I could live with this," he says, pointing to his sightless eyes. Then, with his face glowing with joy, he cries, "Because the last thing I ever saw was the most beautiful sight I could ever live to see — you."[1]

## Lamb-like Beauty

In an infinitely higher way, Jesus — the Lamb of God — is the most beautiful sight you and I could ever live to see. He was beautiful in His pre-incarnate glory, as He offered Himself as the Lamb before the creation of the world. He was beautiful as He presented himself in the types and shadows of the Old Testament, pouring out blood as a lamb on the altar. He was beautiful when He walked this earth in His lamb-like humanity and His lion-like divinity. Though He was the fullness of the Godhead in bodily form, compassion filled Him as He walked in human flesh. He showed us the tears of God spilling from His eyes and dripping down the skin of His cheeks. He showed us the tenderness of God as He ached over lost humanity. He showed us the mercy of God as He yearned over those who rejected Him. But never was He so beautifully displayed as when He hung as the bleeding Lamb on the cross, pouring out mercy and grace and love.

So look at Him now. Focus intently with the eyes of your heart. See love filling every drop of blood. Watch mercy falling in every tear. See compassion burning from His heart. Feel the love swelling in His soul. He loves you so much — it's indescribable!

His love is deeper than the deepest ocean. It is wider than the expanse of the sky. It is higher than the loftiest mountain peak. We can never comprehend the magnitude of His love, but if we will come quietly to Calvary and lift up the eyes of our hearts, we will see, like the blind soldier, the most beautiful sight a person could ever live to see — the Lamb.

Spurgeon made this startling statement to ministers: "Playing with men's souls is murderous work, and truly if the Lamb of God be not preached, the ministry is playing with souls, if not worse."[2] Whether you are preaching, teaching or witnessing, the Lamb should be your central subject — not money, not materialism or prosperity, not lesser subjects. We must cause people to see — with the eyes of their hearts — the crucified Lamb of God.

This was indeed the secret to Paul's ministry. He didn't glory in the miracles of Jesus; he didn't glory in the teachings of Jesus; he didn't glory in the resurrection of Jesus; he didn't glory in the ascension of Jesus or the second coming of Jesus, as wonderful as all these were. Paul said, *"God forbid that I should glory, save in THE CROSS of our Lord Jesus Christ"* (Galatians 6:14, KJV).

Yes, Paul knew that the cross is *"the power of God"* (1 Corinthians 1:18). That's why he *"resolved to know nothing ... except Jesus Christ and Him crucified"*

(1 Corinthians 2:2, NIV). Referring to this verse, Spurgeon said, "Some preachers know too much, and the sooner they join the holy know-nothings the better."[3]

This was indeed Paul's secret. He had the ability to preach so graphically about the Lamb that people could see what he was saying. He said to the Galatians, *"You had Jesus Christ crucified clearly portrayed before your very eyes"* (Galatians 3:1, my paraphrase). The Greek word translated *portrayed* is *prographo*, which means "to paint a picture and lift it up on a public placard."

John R. W. Stott said, "Paul here likens his gospel-preaching either to a huge canvas painting or to a placard publicly exhibiting a notice of advertisement. The subject of his painting or placard was Jesus Christ on the cross."[4]

Stott made this profound statement that every teacher or preacher needs to hear today: "One of the greatest arts or gifts in gospel-preaching is to turn people's ears into eyes, and to make them see what we are talking about."[5] So graphically did Paul describe the wounds, the blood, the pain, the sin, the punishment, the cries of Jesus that it was like he had painted a picture with words.

I know this was the secret of Charles Spurgeon's ministry, but it was also the key to John Wesley's ministry. The cross was his "consuming preoccupation." "It was with the *kerygma* of the Cross that he set out to reach Britain for Christ," said A. Skevington Wood in his classic work on Wesley.[6]

Spurgeon told a story of a team of Moravian missionaries in Greenland who decided they must first explain the nature of Deity, teach right from wrong and prove the need of atonement for sin. For years they labored to prepare the Greenlanders for the Gospel, with nothing to show for their efforts.

Then one day, one of the missionaries happened to read to one of the natives the story of Jesus bleeding on the cross. The Greenlander asked him to read the story again. Then, clapping his hands, the native cried, "Why did you not tell us that before?" Spurgeon cried, "Ah, just so! That is the point to begin with. Let us start with the Lamb of God that takes away the sin of the world."[7]

Steve Hill learned this lesson one day when he was preaching to a group of teenagers in America. He told stories of powerful conversions, but the more he preached, the more the youth acted silly and cut up. Several even mocked the message.

Then the Lord said to Steve, "Preach the blood, Steve. If I be lifted up, I will draw all men unto Me. Speak of My suffering, My pain, My cross." Steve repented quickly for grieving the Holy Spirit and began preaching about the pain and blood and crucifixion of Christ. "Within just a few minutes, my listeners were weeping uncontrollably," he said. "The more I preached the cross, the more they cried."[8]

You see, this generation cannot be reached with wordy, intellectual dogma. But you can reach them with a gripping, graphic, heart-melting revelation of the Lamb. Cause them to see the Pierced One until all lesser subjects fade. As someone said, "Since my eyes were fixed on Jesus, I've lost sight of all beside; so enchained my spirit's vision, gazing on the Crucified."[9]

Martyn Lloyd-Jones said, "There is no end to this glorious message of the cross, for there is always something new and fresh and entrancing and moving and uplifting that one has never seen before."[10]

Indeed, you may ascend the highest snowcapped mountain and view the scene below, but never will you see anything to rival the beauty of the Lamb. Look into the face of the brightest angel or the sweetest child, watch the sun gleam orange folds across a sea at sunrise, but never will you see God's love and grace and glory more perfectly displayed than on a humble little hill outside Jerusalem where the blood of God flowed in scarlet rivers.

Spurgeon described this powerfully:

> *O earth and heaven and hell! O time and eternity, things present and things to come, visible and invisible, you are dim mirrors of the Godhead compared with the bleeding Lamb. O heart of God, I see you nowhere as at Golgotha, where*

*the Word incarnate reveals the justice and the love, the holiness and the tenderness of God in one blaze of glory. If any created mind desires to see the glory of God, he need not gaze upon the starry skies or soar into the heaven of heavens; he has but to bow at the foot of the cross and watch the crimson streams that gush from Immanuel's wounds.*[11]

So magnificent was the scene at Calvary that all nature bowed its head. The sun hid its face. The wind held its breath. The birds hushed their singing. And not until the Lamb released His spirit to the Father did all nature erupt. The whole earth shook in a violent earthquake, the rocks and boulders split apart, and even the graves of some of the dead were opened (see Matthew 27).

It was as though all creation was announcing — "Behold the beauty of the Lamb!" Little wonder, then, that Paul would proclaim so passionately: *"God forbid that I should glory, save in the cross of our Lord Jesus Christ"!* (Galatians 6:14, KJV).

One day in my Systematic Theology class, my students started expressing their disgust that so many preachers leave out the message of the cross. Even if they tell it, they sentimentalize it, not explaining the depths. Someone mentioned that the message of the hour, however, is intimacy with God, not the cross. Suddenly the Holy Spirit hit me with a simple revelation. I said, "Yes, intimacy is the call of the hour, but what happens when you actually come into intimacy with God? What do you see?"

One young man responded, "I would see a light so unapproachable I could hardly bear to look at it!"

I urged them to keep thinking about what they would see if they came into deep communion with the Lord. Eventually, I said, "Let's look through the window of the book of Revelation to see what John saw when he came into intimate fellowship," and we continued.

First, we noted that John saw, standing in the center of the throne, the Lamb, still bearing wounds from the cross (see Revelation 5:6). *"Worthy is the Lamb,"* cried the heavenly beings, for the Lamb was the center of their intimate worship (5:12).

Standing around the throne were people from *"every nation, tribe, people and language,"* and they were all standing *"in front of the Lamb"* (7:9, NIV). Those who sang a new song, the ones who were redeemed among men were those who *"follow the Lamb wherever He goes"* (14:4, NIV). Even the *"new song"* they sing is *"the song of Moses ... and the song of the Lamb"* (15:3, NIV). The shepherd who leads those in Heaven to the living waters is none other than the Lamb (see 7:17).

The high point in Heaven is the wedding of the Lamb, and blessed are those who are invited to the wedding supper of the Lamb (19:7 and 9). We could go on and on, for the Lamb is mentioned at least twenty-nine times in Revelation. The point is that when we truly come into intimacy with God, we will behold the Lamb.

## A Revelation of the Lamb
## Your First Sight in Heaven

When you die, what will be the first sight you see? If Jesus is the Lord of your life on earth, you will open your eyes in Heaven and behold the face of the Lamb. There He will stand, shining in splendor, streams of glory flowing from the piercings in His flesh.

Surely you will fall on your knees at the moment you behold the beauty of the Lamb. Then, just as the blind veteran cried to Colonel Maggie, you will cry, "Jesus, You are truly the most beautiful sight a person could ever live to see!"

**Endnotes:**

1. Susan M. Christianson, cited in Jack Canfield, Mark Victor Hansen, and Sidney R. Slagter, "Colonel Maggie and the Blind Veteran," in *Chicken Soup for the Veteran's Soul*, p. 92.
2. Charles Spurgeon, "Behold the Lamb of God," in *Spurgeon's Expository Encyclopedia*, p. 104.
3. Charles Spurgeon, "Behold the Lamb of God," in *Spurgeon's Expository Encyclopedia*, p. 105.
4. John R. W. Stott, *The Cross of Christ* (Grand Rapids, MI: Baker Book House, 1987), p. 343.
5. John R. W. Stott, *The Cross of Christ*, p. 343.
6. A. Skevington Wood, *The Burning Heart: John Wesley, Evangelist* (Minneapolis: Bethany Fellowship, Inc., 1967), p. 237.

7. Charles Spurgeon, "The Marvelous Magnet," in *The Power of the Cross of Christ*, p. 16.

8. Stephen Hill, *Time to Weep*, p. 48.

9. Walter B. Knight, *Masterbook of New Illustrations* (Grand Rapids, MI: William B. Eerdmans Publishing Company, 1956), p. 722.

10. Martyn Lloyd-Jones, *The Cross* (Westchester, IL: Crossway Books, 1987), p. xiii.

11. Charles Spurgeon, "Mourning at the Sight of the Crucified," in *The Power of the Cross of Christ*, p. 192.

## Six

# The Light of the Lamb on the Throne

Nineteen-year-old Raymond lay unconscious in the snow and mud of Italy during World War II. A mortar had exploded, killing all his buddies. Their bodies now lay strewn around him.

Strangely, he heard a voice. He would know that voice anywhere. It was Mama. She was calling, "Raymond, get up! Get up right now!"

At first, he thought he was back home and Mama was calling him to get up for school. He opened his eyes and realized that he was in Italy. Blood streamed down his face, and he was stone deaf. Confused and in shock, he didn't know where to go for help. He wasn't sure which way was enemy lines or where the Americans were. He felt helpless, panicked.

Then he heard Mama again, speaking sternly, "Raymond, go toward the light! Go toward the light!"

Back home, thousands of miles away, Mama had been awakened from a dream. She shook her husband, crying, "Something has happened to our boy! I dreamed he was calling to me for help. I thought he was a little boy again, and he was crying, so I called to him to get up and come to the light so I could see what was wrong with him." She got up and refused to go back to sleep.

Meanwhile, back in Italy, Raymond stumbled toward the light, not knowing where he was going. As he hobbled around a bend in the road, bleeding from a wound in his leg, he fell into the arms of an American medic.

Shortly afterward, he was shipped home. As he sat with his mother and family at the kitchen table, they both shared what had happened. Tears streamed down both faces as they told their stories of the light.

Raymond told how the medics said it had almost

been too late. "They said that I was lucky to have caught them. They had already searched the area I was in for the wounded, shipping them out first, and then returning for the dead. Had I not regained consciousness and moved toward them, I'd have bled to death from the leg injuries before they found me."

Raymond later married and regained most of his hearing, but he never tired of telling the story. He always ended it by saying, "I was all the way over in Italy, stone deaf, but I heard her all the same. 'Go to the light, Raymond,' she said. 'Go to the light.' I'll never understand how she did it, but it was my mama that saved my life that night — my mama and the light."[1]

Would you let me be like that mama to you right now? Whether you are old or still very young, let me urge you — always go toward the light. God has a river of glory to give you. He has life to pour into your weary soul. He has the energy of the Holy Spirit with which to fill you.

So lift your eyes now to the light. See the One on the throne who shines in ravishing splendor.

Look up once more and see Jesus. See the brilliance that gleams from His countenance. You see, until we behold the light of the Lamb on the throne, we still haven't finished the story.

Open the window of the book of Revelation again and look at the Lamb, *"looking as though it had been slain"* (Revelation 5:6). Watch myriads of angels, the elders and the living creatures cry, *"Worthy is the Lamb!"* (Revelation 5:12).

Why is He so worthy? Their song explains: *"because you were slain, and with your blood you purchased men for God from every tribe and language and people and nation"* (Revelation 5:9, NIV).

Look closely now at this lovely Lamb, standing like a Wounded Man upon the throne. Though a crown of gold wreathes His head, He still bears pierce marks from the thorns which once stuck in His brow. Now, out of these piercings in His head flow light beams of glory, causing His face to shine like the sun, His eyes to blaze like flames of fire, and His head and His hair to glisten as white as snow (see Revelation 1:14 and 16).

Look at His hands and feet. Though He holds seven stars, nail holes still mar His hands and feet. Now, rays of glory stream out of His hands, for *"His brightness was like the sunlight; rays streamed from His hand, and there [in the sunlike splendor] was the hiding place of His power"* (Habakkuk 3:4, AMP).

That's why in Heaven there is no need of the light of the sun, for the Lamb is the lamp in the city of God (see Revelation 21:23, AMP). He radiates with the shekinah of God, for He is *"the sole expression of the glory of God [the Light-being, the out-raying or radiance of the divine]"* (Hebrews 1:3, AMP).

Look now at His side. Though He wears a robe of majesty, His side is gouged open from the blade of the spear. But look more closely, for out of this gaping wound flow currents of power. It's the river of God, just as John said: *"Then the angel showed me the river of the water of life, as clear as crystal, flowing from the throne of God and of the Lamb"* (Revelation 22:1,

NIV). This word *clear* in Greek is *lampros*, meaning "radiant and bright." This is indeed a shining river, flowing from the side of the Lamb.

You see, ever since the closing of the Garden of Eden, God the Father had stored this river in the heart of His Son. Do you know what caused the release of this great flood tide? Look back to the cross to discover the undamming of the river of God.

## *The Divine Eruption*

Look now and hear Jesus groan, *"I thirst!"* A soldier wets His tongue with posca, a cheap vinegar wine. Then Jesus lifts up His lungs and shouts the cry of victory: *"It is finished!"* Just as creation was completed in six days, now, with this sixth word from the cross, redemption is completed.

Now Jesus releases His spirit to the Father. And, even as God rested on the seventh day, He enters His rest with this seventh cry from the cross.

Now it happens. All this time, the heart of the Lamb had been swelling and filling with grief. Finally His heart, so engorged with sorrow, so consumed with love, and so overwhelmed with horror from drinking the Father's cup, can take no more. He releases His spirit to the Father, and His heart bursts open in a divine eruption.

You see, Jesus didn't die of suffocation. Nails didn't kill him. Blood loss didn't take His life. No man murdered Him. He gave up His spirit and died of a ruptured, broken heart.

Watch now as a soldier takes his spear and digs it into the side of Jesus — all the way up to His heart. The River of Life was shielded away from Man by cherubs guarding the way to Eden with flaming swords. But now that River is being released once more in the flow of blood and water as the soldier's spear digs into the heart of the Lamb.

Watch as blood and water flow out separately. Do you know what this means? Physicians today tell us that when red cells separate from the clear serum and accumulate around the pericardium, the lining around the heart, this indicates heart rupture. But even more important, the two separate streams, one of blood and the other of water, show us the release of the river of God. The blood was for cleansing, and the water was for reviving. This is a river of glorious revival.

Again, ever since the closing of Eden, this river of God had been cut off. Where did it go? How could it disappear? This was the river that flowed with life and healing and the power of God. How could it be hidden?

It was hidden in the heart of the Lamb. That's why the cross is the hiding place of God's power. When a spear pierced the Savior's heart, the treasure inside spilled out. It was only a trickle at first, but at Pentecost it came in a flood tide of revival.

## The Presence of God in Revival

Can you see this river? Can you feel it roaring and thundering down from the heart of Christ? If you've ever stood at Niagara Falls and looked up, you've gotten a tiny glimpse of the power of this river. That falls pours and roars and gushes and rushes down over the rocks, causing mists to rise and rainbows to form, and providing energy for a large section of North America. In a much higher way, the river of God flows down from the Lamb, providing the energy of God to this earth. It pours and roars and gushes and rushes, streaming out from the heart of the Lamb.

You see, when revival comes, everything changes. Breathing in the freshness of God's presence stirs hope. It ignites faith. It rekindles joy. It heals pain. It creates a love and a yearning for the Lamb beyond anything you've ever experienced.

Many churches across the land have experienced the omnipresence of God, meaning God's presence in all places at all times, but when revival comes, God's manifest presence sweeps in. This is a tangible manifestation of the Holy Spirit. You can feel Him. Your face burns with the light of His face. Your soul trembles with love. Your heart pounds with conviction. The slightest sin becomes unthinkable because you don't want to do anything to offend the Lord. You love His presence so much that you never want Him to withdraw.

As it did for David, God's presence becomes your bread, your purpose, your reason for living. This is why America needs *a revelation of the Lamb*. We need the river of revival that flows down from the side of the Lamb.

## *Your Highest Calling*

So lift your eyes back up to the Lamb on the throne. Draw a little nearer and look into His eyes. See the tears of love gleaming in His eyes. Tune the ears of your spirit to hear His voice. Like the sound of many waters, He speaks, His words roaring like the thunder of Niagara Falls.

What is He saying? I believe He is calling you to go and cry in the wilderness of a shaking world: "Behold the Lamb of God!"

Some of you think you don't have a ministry. You aren't sure you even have a calling from God. You wonder if God could ever use you. You watch the television ministries, and you secretly wish that you, too, could be known around the world. But don't you see? It's not about your fame. It's not about your ministry. It's all about the fame of the Lamb.

Will you lay all ambition for greatness at the foot of the cross? Will you step into the ministry God called you into before the creation of the world? In light of His supreme sacrifice, will you give *a revelation of the Lamb* to America? Laying aside all the poor examples of ministers clamoring for fame and fortune, will you take up the calling God has always intended for you?

It was John the Baptist's highest calling to proclaim, like a voice crying in the wilderness, "Behold the Lamb of God!" And this is your highest calling as well. Will you cry in the wilderness of this present world, "Behold the Lamb of God"?

## Soak America in the River

But before you lift up the Lamb, you must be full of the river of God. You must have revival so inundating your spirit that it splashes out of you everywhere you go.

So won't you let Him pour His river down upon you? Why not look back up to the Lamb even now? Just like John, who saw this river flowing from the Lamb, ask the Lord to bring this river to you.

Call upon the Holy Spirit, and ask Him to come. Let Him see your thirst, for genuine thirst draws the presence of God. Even as rivers flow down to the dry and low places of this earth, God's river streams down to the lowly and thirsty ones.

Humble yourself and cry to God for the river. Let Him come. Let the river flow. Lean back now and soak and soak and soak in it. Like a thirsty traveler in the middle of a desert, drink from these healing streams. And after you've drunk your fill, promise God that, for the rest of your life, you will flow with His river.

These are the healing streams that Jesus died to give to all the nations of this world. So once you are full, begin to step out and bring this river to America. Soak America in the river of God. This river will set America ablaze and sweep revival from sea to shining sea. It will fill her wounds, heal the scars and cause her to bow and worship in the light of the Lamb on the throne.

**Endnote:**

1. Jack Canfield, Mark Victor Hansen, and Sidney R. Slagter, "The Light," in *Chicken Soup for the Veteran's Soul*, pp. 253-256.

# Seven

# A Transforming Vision of the Lamb

The firefighter's eyes widen, and he stands trans-fixed. There, in the midst of the rubble of the Twin Towers in New York City, lies a perfect cross. The beams, six feet high and four feet wide, bear no scars from being cut or welded. Some of the bolts are still intact. A silver object, the remains of a firefighter's jacket melted into the left side of the cross, glistens in the daylight haze.

Dusting off the cross, Frank Silecchia raises it up as a sign in the midst of so much human suffering. Like a spiraling monument in the smoke-filled ru-ins, here it stands, a powerful symbol, pointing up-ward to God.[1]

In a strange but compelling way, this cross jutting heavenward calls the people of a wounded nation to lift their eyes. It points to the God who loves us and hurts with us and wants to reveal Himself to us.

## The Shaking of America

For one hundred days, the fires at Ground Zero burned. They were finally extinguished on December 19, 2001, but out of these fires, a new nation began to be forged.

That fateful fall morning, in the span of a single hour, the most powerful nation on the face of the earth realized that she was not invincible. Before this, America was too proud and self-sufficient to admit her need for God; now we realize that without God we could not stand.

In the midst of another national tragedy, as the blood of American boys spilled into our soil, Abraham Lincoln penned:

*We have grown in numbers, wealth, and power as no other nation has ever grown; but we have forgotten God. ... We have vainly imagined, in the deceitfulness of our hearts, that all these blessings were produced by some superior wisdom and virtue of our own. Intoxicated with unbroken success, we have become too self-sufficient to feel the necessity of redeeming and persevering grace, too proud to pray to the God who made us.*[2]

Once more, even as the nation shook during the Civil War, America has been shaken to the core. Hopefully, a more humble and dependent America has risen from the smoke and ashes of September 11.

From coast to coast, churches have filled with overflowing crowds. Even secular television programs now interview men and women of faith. As one commentator said, "No one is asking for atheists to interview on their talk shows." Fox News reported that "Americans are rediscovering the power of faith."[3] A clerk at a Barnes and Noble bookstore told me, "We can't keep enough Bibles on the shelf!"

Never before have streets and businesses carried signs saying "God Bless America." Never before have congressmen and congresswomen stood arm in arm to sing "God Bless America." Not in decades has Congress convened to pray and seek the Lord.

Tommy Tenney, in his book *Trust and Tragedy,* said that, along with those who died, something else died in this nation:

> *America's arrogance died that September morning. I pray it will not return. Humility will serve us far better and preserve us far longer than arrogance. The aftermath of a tragedy is a fertile field for the rebirth of humility and dependence on God.*[4]

And yet, already, America seems to have hit the snooze button, rolled over and drifted back off to sleep. That's why we must pray for God to shake America until we awake and fall humbly at the feet of the Lamb.

My pastor, John Kilpatrick, was preaching a revival service in a church in California. The pastor of the church began to pray, "Lord, shake the West

Coast of America!" Suddenly, the building rocked. An earthquake had struck, and for over a minute the church shook. People hit the floor, not only because of the earthquake, but because the power of God hit at the same moment.

But this is precisely what God said would happen: *"Once more I will shake not only the earth but also the heavens"* (Hebrews 12:26, NIV). He went on to speak of removing all that is not founded on the Kingdom of Christ (see verses 27-28). Would you be willing to pray: "Lord, whatever it takes, whatever the cost, shake America and bring her to the feet of the Lamb"?

## Why America Needs This Vision

A.W. Tozer said, "To regain her lost power, the Church must see Heaven opened and have a transforming vision of God."[5] I earnestly believe America, too, needs to see Heaven opened and have a transforming vision of the Lamb, and I want to give you now the three primary reasons that America needs this transforming view. They are (1) to experience God's love, (2) to melt in true repentance and (3) to receive a baptism of revival fire.

## To Experience God's Love

Earlier generations sometimes insisted on doctrines without power, truth without anointing, theology without experience, but this left America cold. Today's postmodern generation must have an experience with God.

We must have doctrine on fire, truth empowered by the presence of God, theology aflame with the Holy Spirit. We need to feel the tangible reality of God. We need to experience the love of the Lord, pouring down from Heaven and filling our thirsty hearts.

This is not mere emotionalism, as critics have implied. It's emotion that burns from the heart of God. Our God is supremely emotional. Our own human emotions are tiny drops from the ocean of God's infinite emotions.

That's why *a revelation of the Lamb* is so needed. We need to see the One who loves so much that He bleeds. We need to glimpse the One who yearns over us until hot tears burn His face. We need to see the One who prayed so hard that He literally was sweating blood. We need to experience the One who opens up His heart and pours out rivers of redeeming love.

That's why we need a spiritual encounter with the Lamb. Nobody else loves us like Jesus loves us. He hung on two stakes of wood, as His blood dripped out, so that He could draw us close to Him. He didn't just take our sin upon Himself; He took our punishment for sin. To fully experience the rich floods of the infinite love of God, America needs *a revelation of the Lamb*.

## To Melt in Repentance

We need to encounter God's love, but we also need *a revelation of the Lamb* so our hearts can melt in true repentance. Not until Thomas saw the risen

Christ, still bearing wounds from His crucifixion, did he fall to his knees and cry, *"My Lord and my God!"* Not until Isaiah saw the Lord high and lifted up did he see his own sin. Not until Job saw God with his spiritual eyes did he cry out in deep repentance.

America needs *a revelation of the Lamb* to bring us to our knees and cause us to cry, like Thomas did, "My Lord and my God!" We need a vision of the Lamb so that, like Isaiah, we can moan, *"Woe is me, for I am undone. ... For my eyes have seen the King, the Lord of hosts"* (Isaiah 6:5). We need to see the Lamb so that we can cry, like Job cried, *"I heard of you with my ear, but now I have seen you, and I repent in dust and ashes!"* (Job 42:5-6, my paraphrase). America needs to see the Lord, so we can be swept clean with a spirit of repentance.

Yet many Americans bristle at the mere mention of sin and repentance. Why is that? One reason is that we haven't shown them the Lamb. How long has it been since you've heard a heart-melting sermon on the sacrifice of Calvary, other than at Easter? How deeply have you looked for yourself at the wounds, the cries, the cup Jesus drank?

If you are a teacher or a preacher, does the crucified Lamb permeate your teaching or preaching, as it did Paul's (see 1 Corinthians 2:2)? Charles Spurgeon said, "The preacher's principal business, I think I might say, his only business, is to cry, 'Behold the Lamb of God!' "[6]

Above all, the Church needs a fresh revelation of the Lamb so that she can stand in the gap for the sins of the nation and repent. Then, with blood-washed souls and hearts bursting with compassion, we can step forward to bring *a revelation of the Lamb* to America. It's a revelation that will ultimately bring a nation to her knees in true repentance.

## To Receive Revival Fire

But our nation also needs to behold the Lamb so that she can receive a mighty baptism of the Holy Spirit and fire. John the Baptist preached his finest sermon the day he pointed to Jesus and cried: *"Behold! The Lamb of God!"* (John 1:29). But after this revelation of the Lamb came his next greatest sermon:

*"He will baptize you with the Holy Spirit and fire!"* (Matthew 3:11 and Luke 3:16).

America needs a baptism of fire that will sweep the country with revival. It will come by beholding the Lamb. We need to look up at Jesus until Heaven opens and revival descends like sparks from the altar. We need to feel the hot flecks showering down upon us until the dry tinder of our hearts ignites with revival fire.

On September 14, 2001, speaking at the National Cathedral in Washington, Billy Graham remarked, "One of the things we desperately need is a spiritual renewal in this country. We need a spiritual revival in America."

Revival has already come to the shores of North America. It started several years ago in certain wellheads, such as Brownsville, Toronto and Pasadena. If you have traveled to an oasis of revival, you know the wonder of soaking your heart in the warm streams of His presence. Nothing so heals, so refreshes, so fills with unspeakable joy as drenching yourself in the presence of God in revival.

Once you have tasted the sweetness of God's presence, hunger will ache in your soul. Thirst will burn in your being. Having breathed in the rich atmosphere of Heaven, your heart will yearn and groan for more and more of Him. You will cry, "Give me revival or I die!"

But will you cry this for America? Rachel cried, *"Give me children, or else I die!"* (Genesis 30:1). John Knox cried, "Give me Scotland or I die!" May you be one who lifts your voice to Heaven and cries, "Give me revival for America or I die!"

Yes, our nation needs *a revelation of the Lamb* that will fill us with redeeming love, melt us in true repentance and baptize us in revival fire.

## *Take a Long Look, America!*

A former slave lifted up her little girl, as a train, carrying the flag-draped casket of Abraham Lincoln, passed by. "Take a long look, Honey!" she cried. "That's the man who died to set you free!"[7]

This is what we need to do today in our country.

We need to call America to take a long, intent look at the Man in Heaven who died to set us free. We need to see Heaven opened and have a vision of the Lamb. In this hour of dying hopes and shattered dreams, this is what we must have.

So I challenge you: Give America *a revelation of the Lamb*. Our nation is open and tender right now. Americans need to hear about Jesus, but please don't give them a shallow, memorized, mechanical message. Former generations were persuaded by information, but postmodern generations must experience God. They must see Him. They must feel Him. They must have the real, the authentic. They need to see the bleeding Lamb.

So show them Jesus. Call them to behold the Pierced One. Turn their ears into eyes as they see the Lamb, dripping with blood and roaring in agony as He drinks the Father's cup.

Pray your heart out in private so that when you lift up the Lamb they will experience the river of God. Lead them into His presence. Cause them to experience revival because you've been on your face pleading with God for an outpouring.

Indeed, it is high time to inject hope into the bloodstream of our nation. It's time to transfuse her vessels with the blood drawn from the veins of the Lamb. It's time to call America to look up and see a transforming vision of the Lamb.

**Endnotes:**

1. "Firefighter's Cross Stands Tall Amid Rubble," *Maranatha Christian* in *Journal*, October 30, 2001, online story of Frank Silecchia at Ground Zero.
2. Abraham Lincoln (March 30, 1863), "Lincoln's Prayer Proclamation," in *America Out of the Ashes*, p. 217.
3. Janet Chismar, "God Returns to America's Public Square," in *America Out of the Ashes*, p. 203.
4. Tommy Tenney, *Trust and Tragedy: Encountering God in Times of Crisis* (Nashville: Thomas Nelson Publishers, 2001), p. 103.
5. A.W. Tozer, The *Knowledge of the Holy: The Attributes of God: Their Meaning in the Christian Life* (San Francisco: Harper & Row Publishers, 1961), p. 121.
6. Charles H. Spurgeon, "Behold the Lamb," in *Spurgeon's Expository Encyclopedia,* Vol. 3 (Grand Rapids, MI: Baker Book House, 1977), p. 103.
7. Janet Chismar, "God Returns to America's Public Square," in *America Out of the Ashes*, p. 205.

# Eight

# *The Presence of the Lamb for America*

A bride waited on the steps of the church, her eyes searching the streets. Both her father and grandfather had died that same year. Her only brother, a firefighter, had promised to walk her down the aisle, but he, too, had died, of a heart attack while fighting fires shortly before the wedding. Now Mayor Rudy Giuliani, the man who kept New York City from falling apart, had promised to stand in for her brother. In a neighborhood where over two dozen firefighters were missing and presumed dead, his presence at the wedding would ignite a spark of joy.

Suddenly, a crowd lining the street outside the church erupted with cheers. The mayor had come, just as he promised. Grinning broadly, Rudy slipped up to the bride and cradled her arm in his. As he proudly strode down the aisle, escorting the bride to her bridegroom, the congregation in the church burst into tearful applause.

"It was phenomenal that he came," cried one of the bridesmaids. "God bless you, Rudy!" cried another. "That's a great thing the mayor did, to give us something happy to come and see in the midst of all this tragedy," said a lady whose son was one of the fallen heroes.[1]

Indeed, the presence of this gallant mayor brought joy in the midst of sorrow and healing to an entire city. But I want to tell you there is another One whose presence can heal this entire nation. Now America's greatest need is the presence of the Lamb.

## *The Power of His Presence*

Chapel ends at Brownsville Revival School of Ministry, and students are invited to come forward. Music flows on, "You are the air I breathe. ... I'm desperate for You!" I open my eyes to take in the scene. Young men and women kneel at the altar pouring their hearts out to God. Many lie on their faces sobbing. Others crowd forward, their hands stretched as high as they can reach, as though reaching up to touch the face of God.

Worship continues. The presence of God floods the sanctuary even more. The Holy Spirit flows down on every student. The whole room is charged with the Spirit of God. It's as though the river of God has rushed down from above, filling the chapel with glory. Breathing in this air is like inhaling the atmosphere of Heaven. No one wants to leave this holy presence.

The staff and faculty walk through the crowd, laying hands on students. We are merely blessing what God is already doing. As I pray, I am aware that the reason the presence of God fills this place is all because of the Lamb. Because He drank the Father's cup and allowed His heart to burst open on the cross, now a river of His presence flows down on His people. This is the atmosphere of glory He wants to pour down on churches everywhere. He wants to flood America with a river of revival, flowing down from the wounds of the Lamb.

It was here in this chapel, just a few months earlier, that the Lord first told me, "America needs *a revelation of the Lamb*." Now, as the Spirit of God streams out over the students, I think, *O Lord, this is truly what America needs*.

America needs to feel the warm power of God's presence settling down from Heaven. She needs to breathe in the freshness of the Holy Spirit. She needs the spirit of revival injected into her veins, infusing life through the bloodstream of this great nation. And once she has experienced these refreshing streams, nothing else will satisfy.

## "A Revelation of My Son"

One night while I was worshiping at Brownsville, where a river of revival flows richly, the Lord spoke to me. It was similar to the word He had given in chapel a few days after 9/11. Resounding out of Heaven and filling my spirit came the phrase:

*A revelation of My Son as the Lamb!*
*A revelation of My Son as the Lamb!*
*A revelation of My Son as the Lamb!*

With a sense of divine urgency, over and over He repeated this to my hungry, listening heart. It was one simple phrase, but I knew in a flash what this meant.

I could feel the longing in the Father's heart. He yearns for His Son to receive the glory He deserves for what He suffered on the cross. For centuries, He has watched the Church turn aside from the cross, only bringing it out of a dusty corner once a year, at Easter.

I sensed the Father's urgent desire to reveal His Son as the Lamb to the Church so she could be purified and could ultimately reveal Him to America. Indeed, a revelation of the Son as the Lamb will purge unholy motives from the Church. It will cause passion for God to burn. It will dissolve hidden motives for power and position, money and fame. It will wipe away desires for vainglory and for honor from people. It will break our hearts with that which breaks the heart of God.

A revelation of the Son as the Lamb will cause us to flame with a passion for souls. This was why He gave Himself as the Lamb. Jesus said, *"The Son of Man came to seek and to save what was lost"* (Luke 19:10, NIV). A revelation of the Son as the Lamb will send us into the streets, onto the college and university campuses, into the schools and prisons *"to seek and to save"* the lost. It will cause our hearts to pound with the heartbeat of Heaven — the passion for lost souls.

A revelation of the Son as the Lamb will cause us to feel what He feels for the poor. We've sat on our comfortable pews, growing fatter by the year, while thousands shiver in the shadows of the inner cities of America, hungry, homeless, forgotten. A revelation of the Son as the Lamb will send us to the streets to feed and clothe the poor.

A revelation of the Son as the Lamb will heal the racial scars on the soul of America. For, as John Dawson tells us, bleeding wounds may heal with time, but bleeding hearts do not.[2] A revelation of the

Son as the Lamb will lead us to humble ourselves in true repentance. We will see the walls of division between the races melting in warm tears of repentance and reconciliation.

A revelation of the Son as the Lamb will bring the Church into unity like that of the Church in Heaven, whose members are *"from every nation, tribe, people and language"* (Revelation 7:9, NIV). When at last the world sees this kind of unity in the Church, people will be drawn irresistibly to the Lamb.

## The Coming Flood Tide

When I worship at Brownsville, something amazing happens. In the spirit, I see Jesus as the Lamb with floods and floods and floods of revival flowing from His wounds. Revival is not receding; it is flooding out more and more, and we are about to experience an explosion of this flood tide.

In 1995, I saw the same vision when revival first touched my life. I was attending Harvest Rock Church at Mott Auditorium while in seminary in

Pasadena, California. On my first visit, I went forward, with skepticism, for ministry. A lady on the ministry team lifted her hand and prayed, "More, Lord!" I don't think she even touched me, but the Holy Spirit did. I hit the floor, sobbing.

When I finally sat up, I suddenly had a vision of the Lord. I saw Jesus with floods and floods and floods of revival streaming from Him. With this vision came this scripture, *"He will come like a pent-up flood that the breath of the* LORD *drives along"* (Isaiah 59:19, NIV). In an instant, I understood that the revival God was pouring out was flowing from the Lamb Himself. Now that same view fills my vision as I worship the Lamb at Brownsville.

One reason God pours out such a powerful presence of His Spirit on Brownsville is the emphasis on repentance, salvation of souls and the cross. The messages of Steve Hill, and now of other leading evangelists, always bring hundreds of souls to the altar and break them at the feet of the Lamb.

The ministry school has courses anchored in the cross, with a strong emphasis on repentance and holiness. Students burn with a passion for holiness, fleeing the slightest hint of sin. They hit the streets weekly, leading souls to the Lamb.

Another reason I believe God continues to pour out sustained revival at Brownsville is that Pastor John Kilpatrick loves God's presence more than life itself. When he was an eight-year-old boy, God promised him that He would be a Father to him. Having been abandoned and rejected by his own father, young Kilpatrick went after God with all his heart. Now the presence of the Lamb is his highest priority, and the whole world comes here to Pensacola to drink from this flowing river.

## A River of Glory for America

You see, there is a river tumbling down from the Lamb of God on the throne (see Revelation 22:1). The river flows from Him and through Him and back to Him. Even as rivers flow down to the thirsty places of this earth, the river of God flows down to those who are thirsty. And just as a river seeks to flow back to its source in the ocean, the river of God carries us back to its source in the heart of the Lamb.

This is what our nation desperately needs. America needs the river of God. She needs to have her bleeding wounds healed, her faith rekindled, her passions inflamed, her feelings quickened, her emotions stirred. America needs the presence of the Lamb.

In every corner of this country — from the alabaster cities of the northeast, to the plains of America's heartland, to the purple mountains of the west, to the cotton fields and oil wells of the south — from sea to shining sea — America needs the Lamb.

God shed His grace on America so that we could be a nation shining as a beacon to the world. He wanted us to be a nation where men and women of all races would be free to worship Him.

God has used America, the most powerful nation in the world, to help to protect Israel and to crush the scourges of Nazism and Communism in the twentieth century. Now in the twenty-first century,

He is using America to stand with Israel and rid the world of terrorism. But we cannot succeed without God. *A revelation of the Lamb* will keep our nation humble and dependent on Him.

And though towers may fall, planes may crash, markets may plummet and darkness may increase upon this earth, the glory of the Lord will increase upon His people (see Isaiah 60:1-3). Even now, as our Redeemer draws nearer, His presence precedes Him. Like the rays of the sun that preview the sunrise, the rivers of splendor spill out from the wounds of the Lamb. Already, we can feel the rays warming our faces. Our hearts race, and our spirits pant for the presence of the Lamb.

So look up one more time at Jesus. There He is, standing like a slain Lamb, shining in ascension glory, receiving our sweet adoration.

Look closely at Him now. His eyes, which once swam with tears on the cross, now flash with blazing fire. His hair, once drenched with bloody sweat, now gleams with lightning-white brilliance. His body, once shamefully beaten and stripped, is now robed in spendor. His face, once soaked with human spit, now shines with sun rays of glory. His hands that bled from nail wounds now stream with light beams of power. His feet, once bolted to a stake of wood, now gleam like burnished brass. His side, once pierced with a soldier's spear, now issues forth rivers of revival.

There in Heaven He stands, like a slain Lamb, bursting with currents of light. I believe that He longs to discharge this fountain of glory down upon America.

## My Prayer for You

A few months after 9/11, I found myself at the school of ministry's graduation. It was like nothing I'd ever seen. At one point, students came forward and knelt. The faculty walked around laying hands on each student. As I touched each student, I prayed the vision God had put on my heart. I prayed that God would impart to them *a revelation of the Lamb*.

Now, as we come to the end of this little book, I

pray this same prayer for you. You have read through these pages, and I believe the Holy Spirit has already forged *a revelation of the Lamb* in your heart. Now I pray:

> *Come, Holy Spirit. Please impart to this hungry one a vision of the Lamb of God that will never fade. Let a view of His flowing wounds be forever painted on this heart. May a vision of the Lamb, drinking the Father's cup and taking our punishment for sin, cause this spirit to never cease trembling.*
>
> *Now I pray that You will drench this seeking soul with the life-giving streams of the river of God. Come, Holy Spirit, and pour revival down upon this thirsty one. Soak this longing soul with the healing streams that pour from the wounds of the Lamb.*

Now, open wide, and let God fill you and fill you and fill you some more. Be forever gripped by the vision of the Lamb, for you can only give to others what He has given to you. May you spend the rest of your life calling others to see the Lord. Let them behold the Lamb until rivers from His heart flow down on them.

And now, join me as we cry to God for America:

> *O God, we plead with You to save America! Forgive us for our pride, our materialism, our immorality and our self-sufficiency, and help us to become a nation wholly dependent on You.*
>
> *Have mercy on our nation, and send revival to America! Let the hole torn open in the side of the Lamb bring floods and floods and more floods of Your river to this nation. Let Your river of revival sweep over this country and cover the land from sea to shining sea.*

In a moment, I would like for you to close this book and kneel down at the feet of the Lamb. Reach up and kiss the wounds in His hands and feet. Let Him feel your love as you tell Him:

*O Lord, it is my highest motive and deepest passion to bring glory to You for giving Your life as the Lamb. For the rest of my life, everything I do will flow out of this grand vision. Until I breathe my last breath, I will lift You up and give America a GRAND REVELATION OF THE LAMB!*

*Amen!*

**Endnotes:**
1. Steve Lopez, "A Promise Kept Brings Joy in the Midst of Sorrow," in *America Out of the Ashes*, pp. 111-115; originally printed in *The Los Angeles Times*, 2001.
2. John Dawson, "Healing America's Wounds: A Call to Repentance and Reconciliation" video, Global Net Productions, 1998.